AVALANCHE: A SURVIVAL GUIDE

These poems, so obviously worthy of high praise, are made of sterner stuff than the breezy, philosophical wanderings of much in today's poetry. Where Harkness finds his attention drawn, he draws our attention, and does so quietly, without a lot of intellectual gimmickry. *Avalanche* is indeed a survival guide, in the highest sense: these poems offer a way to see the world that honors all of our human complexities, and they do so with an attention to sound and detail that rewards our closest engagement.

~Dennis Held, author of *Not Me, Exactly* and *Betting on the Night*

Ed Harkness is a seasoned traveler on our planet and *Avalanche: A Survival Guide* gives us a brilliant collection of his insights in poems by turn fierce, tender, and filled with the richest of details: glimpses of nature, including birds, trees and beaches, details of people from old, remembered relatives to a newborn grandchild. Tone perfect, accurate, musical and surprising, these poems enrich with rereading. The final poem, from the point of view of Raven (inspired by a Tony Angell sculpture), ends on a perfect note:
"That's where we are now. The good news: we're free.
The bad news: we're free to do harm to ourselves, to each other."
He concludes: "Listen. / He squawks his heart out into the blue silence of the sky."
Read these passionate and necessary poems.

~Patricia Clark, author of *The Canopy* and, most recently,
Self-Portrait with a Million Dollars

Place is a character in these poems, both in the history and natural beauty of the Pacific Northwest and around the world. But these poems are not mere celebrations of beauty. In "F-16 Flyby over Bridal Veil Falls" "The trail tunneled through pine and hemlock shade" where the sounds are "Green hum, branch wince, cone fall." This seemingly timeless setting is fragile, assaulted suddenly by a sonic boom. Sometimes subtly, sometimes fiercely in other poems, Harkness brings home the state of our world—racism, shootings, destruction—because these things cannot be ignored. As in the title poem, life can take an abrupt turn at any moment, yet the response is not passive; the response is to look fearlessly because perseverance with spirit is itself a triumph.

~Sherry Rind, author, most recently, of *The Store-House of Wonder and Astonishment*

Also by Edward Harkness

The Law of the Unforeseen, poems, Pleasure Boat Studio press, 2018
Beautiful Passing Lives, poems, Pleasure Boat Studio press, 2010
Saying the Necessary, poems, Pleasure Boat Studio press, 2000
Ice Children, a poetry chapbook, Split Lip Press, 2014
Syringa in Twilight, a poetry chapbook, Red Wing Press, 2010
Watercolor Painting of a Bamboo Rake, A Heron's Eye Chapbook,
    (an affiliate *of* Brooding Heron Press), 1993
Fiddle Wrapped in a Gunnysack, a poetry chapbook, Dooryard Press, 1984
long eye lost wind forgive me, a poetry chapbook, Copperhead Press
    (an imprint of Copper Canyon Press), 1975

Avalanche: A Survival Guide

POEMS

Edward Harkness

Avalanche: A Survivor's Guide

Blue Cedar Press PO Box 48715
Wichita, KS 67201
Visit the Blue Cedar Press website: www.bluecedarpress.com
10 9 8 7 6 5 4 3 2 1

First edition August 2023
ISBN: 978-1-958728-15-4 (paper)
Library of Congress Control Number: 2023944360

Cover photo by author
Design and layout by Gina Laiso, Integrita Productions
Editor Michael Poage

Section i. Spring: In spring-time...a song from As You Like It, is, like all
of Shakespeare's works, in the public domain.
The trees are coming...by Philip Larkin from "High Windows" in
Collected Poems, edited by Anthony Thwaite, published by Farrar,
Straus, Giroux, 1989, p. 166. Section ii. Winter: Tonight as it gets cold...
by Mark Strand from "Lines in Winter," from Selected Poems,
published by Atheneum, 1980, p. 117.
"Breath," by Tess Gallagher, from Is, Is Not, published by Graywolf
Press, 2019, p. 99. Section iii. Fall: November always... From an 1864
letter by Emily Dickinson to her friend, Elizabeth Holland. Section iv.
Summer Hot town, summer...from the song "Summer in the City," by
The Lovin' Spoonful. Release date: July 4, 1966. Lyrics by John Sebas-
tian, Mark Sebastian, and Steve Boone. Section v. Future Spring: I wake
from dreams...by the Song Dynasty poet, Li Qingzhao (1084-1155), from
As Though Dreaming: Tz'u of Pure Jade, translated from the Chinese by
Lenore Mayhew and William McNaughton, Mushinsha Press, 1977. Li
is often regarded as one of the greatest Chinese poets, in the company of
the luminaries of Tang Dynasty poetry: Du Fu, Li Bai and Wang Wei.

Printed in the United States of America

Dedication

For the fam: Linda, Devin and Ned; Randy Harkness, Cindy Howard, Megan Kohl, Lyndsey Mackenzie; and the Three Muses, Clio, Hilde and Cosmo

In memory of Doris Harkness, 1926 - 2023

TABLE OF CONTENTS

i
SPRING

In spring-time, the only pretty ring-time,
When birds do sing, hey ding a ding, ding,
Sweet lovers love the spring.

SHAKESPEARE's *AS YOU LIKE IT*, ACT 5, SCENE 3

The trees are coming into leaf
Like something almost being said;
The recent buds relax and spread,
Their greenness is a kind of grief.

FROM "THE TREES," BY PHILIP LARKIN

The Big Project

Two sawhorses, a yard-sale hollow core door – my backyard worktable.
On it, a pawnshop of tools: chop-saw, cat's paw, level, cordless drill, square,

nail apron in whose pockets are – yes – nails; also tape, carpenter's pencil
a peach pit. Ear protectors, eye protectors, gloves – all close at hand

for my big project: a doghouse. I have no dog. That said, I make a racket—
hammer whacks, gargle of the drill, shrieks of bloody murder from the saw.

In the silent spaces between board cuts, ear protectors tossed aside,
I hear a tiny tapping, rapid fire bursts from a delicate machine gun.

They're barely audible. Pause. Burst of taps. Pause. Burst of taps.
From where? At which point I notice crumbs of wood float down

from the cherry tree. Of course. Woodpecker, this one a tiny Downy,
back of the head red-patched, a dozen paces from where I stand.

He has chiseled in the trunk a hole no larger than a quarter—
excavating a pocket in the heart of the tree. It so happens

a female Downy has just hit town. She clings to the trunk
above the nest-builder. She doesn't give him the time of day,

pulling disinterestedly at a bit of moss. He taps away. She dashes off
as if the prospects might be better elsewhere. He calls it a day,

then rockets in her direction. That's how it is. You work at a project
with the tools at hand. You hope someone finds your creation—

a nest in a cherry tree, a doghouse *sans* dog, a17-foot tall marble statue
of a naked man with a sling – interesting, worthwhile, a home-made gift,

utilitarian, sturdy, or, if not, ephemeral as moonlight on a frog pond.
The Downy chicks have long since fledged. Even now, in the silent

spaces of my life, I hear the pleasing taps of a woodpecker,
a sculptor's chisel. It's called *creation*. It's what we creatures do.

PACHELBEL'S *CANON IN D*

She's off in the junk room to try her hand
once more on the used upright gotten free
from Craigslist. No one wants old pianos.

She'd rather I didn't listen, which is
why I'm listening from the kitchen sink.
She makes small mistakes, urging her fingers

to recall the old dance steps on the keys
decades since she played Pachelbel by heart.
Played by heart – that sweet sad phrase for knowing

a piece well enough you don't have to think,
only to learn the mind takes out the trash,
discards threadbare passions, old skills, old dreams.

Still, she can finger well enough to let
Pachelbel's notes spill forth like April rain,
a waterfall of tumbling chords, major

to minor, back again to major, then
up to high D, falling down, falling up—
a pattern like sunset, moonrise, summer,

winter, years, always varied, always the same.
Despite the mistakes, the many restarts,
despite her arthritic hands, two dead keys,

despite this harsh imperfect world and my
struggle to scrub burnt tuna casserole
from a cast-iron skillet, her *Canon*

in D makes its faint way to the kitchen.
I dry the skillet, hang it on its hook
and dab my eyes with the same damp towel.

On Learning a Friend's House Burned to the Ground

To lose all to flame,
your life become sodden ash,
is to lose all but your name,
Make your one last wish.

Tear out stitches to that hour
before the first blue spark
jumped from the bad wire
in the attic's implacable dark.

A friend says you lost your library—
shelves of art history,
Chinese calligraphy,
a wall of poetry—

including your own—
by my count nine volumes,
still in boxes, now wind-blown.
Two-lives-in-one such fire consumes.

The flames took a book *I* wrote,
my gift to you a life ago,
poems no more consequent
than a patch of spring snow.

What does sorrow have to say?
The world doles out catastrophe
every hour of every day
to those we'll never know or see.

How does anyone bear the weight
of such a loss? Friend, you suffer
the death of words, a vacant heart.
Words are all I have to offer.

THE YEAR OF THE PLAGUE: A LETTER

Isolation. Cold word, with ice in its veins,
not to mention that final syllable, *shun*,
a dark echo. I think of all those rhymed
relatives: nation, duration, desolation,
ovulation, creation – dozens
of cousins, those blood relations
bound to us by skeins of sound.

Alone, cut off from you, loves,
there's not much to do but study
a patch of jonquils, seven in all,
half-hidden by an upturned wheelbarrow
at the corner of the toolshed,
their white sockets frilled, rain-spotted,
splashed by in-and-out sun.

Why have I, after all these years,
only now noticed them? Who,
before we came on the scene,
planted them in this out-of-the-way spot?
In isolation, there can be solace,
even as the dying die alone,
even as the dead have no place

to rest, exhausted by their tribulation.
Then there are the other dead,
the red-caps crammed in the town square
howling approval when the king
waves his rubbery arms, shrugs and grins,
ripping sense from every ruined sentence,
spitting back nonsense to wild applause.

I'm thankful for a certain kind
of solitary confinement, the kind
where we're close by being far.
Here, then, are seven jonquils.
Here's sunlight on their flared skirts.
I give you their stillness, their brief lives.
I give you the breeze that makes them nod.

"Half-breeds Not Otherwise Counted"

Thus, in the florid script of 1870—
ink now well-faded – the census taker
for King County, Washington Territory,
has listed my ancestors on a page titled
"Half-breeds not otherwise counted."

The names have blurred – a flock of starlings
lost in fog. One clear name: "Mathilda,"
age one year. On the line above, Mary,
her mother, 18, surname illegible—
another lost bird. I know these two names.

Thus, in the florid script of 1870
are my kin accounted for, more or less,
in the mundane archives of life on earth,
with its cave paintings, pyramids, gods,
computers, WMDs, self-driving cars.

Somewhere along the line, Mathilda,
age 15, marries a Swede – something Lindstrom,
a fisherman, owner of a skiff to skim
the turgid waters of the Duwamish River,
netting sockeyes and silvers. Back then,

the river hummed clear, bright as quartz.
I'll never know what Mathilda looked like.
Her skin would have been tawny, cedar-
hinted, her hair night-sky dark and thick.
Even at one, her eyes would be hungry,

bright as her Haida mother's, opened wide
to taste the colors and sounds of the world,
to drink in the new thing called light—
łúkwał, in Lushootseed, a tongue
she may have never learned or even heard.

In 1911, Mathilda, now 41,
lays herself down on a mat of ferns
in trees above the beach. She hears
voices of birds, the green song of moss
on alders. She hears Lindstrom

just offshore call to the salmon in Swedish,
kom lax, Lindstrom baling the skiff
with a coffee tin, hauling hand-over-hand
a net to draw in his catch. Gulls whirl
in a frenzy of sobs above his head.

Thus does Mathilda die in the twilight
of a slack tide, childless, in the vicinity
of Point No-Point. She hears the tide turn,
hears Lindstrom's broken whisper,
My darling, must you leave so soon?

Thus, in the florid script of 1870, is Mathilda,
now and for all time, listed on a page titled
"Half-breeds not otherwise counted." I've revised
the page to include a one-year-old girl's eyes,
opened wide to drink in the new thing called light.

WILD IRISES

You were heavy then with our first child.
Those March mornings, before you rose,
I'd go out in the chill of predawn.
I'd step over a strand of barbed wire
from a broken fence rail, hike toward
Takashi's barn, the weeds frost-glazed,
the barn's roof half collapsed.
I'd sit on the lip of a claw-foot bathtub
meant to water, I supposed, Takashi's horses
before the full force of the Depression
wiped out their produce farm. After Pearl Harbor,
so I heard, Takashi, his folks, sisters, wife,
and their four kids, were herded
into the concentration camp in Puyallup.

I'd wait for sunup, there on Takashi's tub,
for a field of wild irises to turn blue.
I'd wait for the tops of three great cottonwoods,
just leafing out, to catch the sun's fire.
The irises would rise, shimmer,
ruffled into a haze of smoke, lake-like.
I'd imagine how I would describe them
to you – A lake of smoke, I'd say,
riffled by sunlight, Takashi's field
flooded by flowers, me in the tub.

You'd have set a fire in the cook-stove,
ground the coffee to the snap
of pine chunks ablaze in the grate.
We had a cable coil table then,
its knotty pine top sanded and oiled.
We'd talk of the birth, excited, not a little
befuddled by having created a new being.

How can we have been that young?
I still see Takashi's fallen barn,
the early spears of camas before
their flowering, the sunlit irises
pale as the sky at that hour.
There's the bathtub. There's me

sitting on it, shivering at sunup,
the iron claw legs long gone to rust.
There's you in a chair near the heat
of the stove, your bathrobe open,
your breasts large, your round belly
aglow, sweat-sheened, ready for its labor
in those last brittle days of winter.

We lived in a two-room rental then,
past the clapboard church, its cross toppled,
belfry empty, on the end of a gravel road.
Now, in July heat, no sign of the broken
fence rail, no barbed wire marking Takashi's
pasture, not one gray board from the barn.
In its place, a convenience store and gas pump.
Out back, the weeds are hip high where, before
our time, his horses would step from the barn
into the sunlight to graze on blue flowers,
to drink from the clawfoot tub I've spent
an hour searching for, gone without a trace.

Being and Unbeing

They aren't young, the young old couple.
How they worked, how hard the soil
had been, soil of their years together.

And here is the blue sea before them,
lines of pelicans, their broad wings winging
mere inches above the waves.

They could no longer be at home
in the old country, could no longer live
with the cruelties, the history book of lies.

A thousand miles they drove their van
to the seaside town with a name
tasting of rum and lime.

They put a down payment on a lot.
They hire a local contractor,
a team of local workers to lay a foundation

on a bluff of leveled compacted sand
well above high tide. Behind the beach,
a forest of papayas, fruited with parrots.

The cinderblocks have been mortared.
Unglazed windows inhale the salt air.
No roof yet. No bed. Mattress on the floor.

They're dirty, sweaty after a day
of pushing wheelbarrows brimmed
with topsoil to the garden plot.

They give each other a sponge bath.
In bed, he massages her calves.
He dies in his sleep,

as she has discovered this morning.
Death, we forget, is never far.
There's nothing more to add

but minor details: drifting off,
content with the day's progress,
soothed by the muffled clap of breakers,

happy in the sight of stars
between open rafters, he taps her bare arm.
Is that Cygnus? Yes, she says, the Swan.

Later, while she slept, he rose,
stepped across the threshold and entered
the unfinished room of unbeing.

Bamboo After Rain

I had to find a magnifying glass to peer inside
each prismatic drop clinging to a leaf tip.

In them, I saw an inverted world
bright with trees, houses, parted clouds,

a neighbor's upside-down parked car.
Give these pure clear planets another hour

to live, if in no other way than by this note
I write on a November night, many months

since my morning study of rain after a May
downpour, followed by a sunbreak.

Time, too, evaporates, then returns as clouded
memory, so it's May once more, in November.

Squinting through the lens. I can't take my eye
off one drop in particular. There's my eye!

It's huge, mirrored, glaring at me
as if my eye is the subject of my eye.

Tonight's forecast: clear and cold.
Once again, I'm in two places at once.

In my hand, I hold a magnifying glass
an inch or so from a drop of rain.

May sun warms the side of my face.
Underfoot, the grass bristles with frost.

Winter stars fan out above the steam
of my breath. That *zzzttt* sound you hear

is the zipper of my parka pulled up.
We may get snow by morning.

Something I've never seen till now:
light drying on the tips of bamboo leaves.

Something I've never seen till now:
the moons of Jupiter with my naked eye.

SPRING IN HANGZHOU

~Li Qingzhao, Song Dynasty poet, 1084-1155 A.D.

Li Qingzhao, you lean
against the plum tree, blossoms
dropped on your shoulder,

your face once more flushed
with wine. Your silk robe, sleeves frayed,
has seen better days.

Mingcheng rose some hours
before you woke. By this time
he's on a boat bound

for the capitol
to fix some political
mess of the ill-read

emperor and his
sycophants. Has beauty died?
Your hair, once ink black,

shows the first touches
of silver. You're cursed to write
poems till dawn, each one

a meticulous
four-character, four-toned song
you sing to the mists.

The cries of wild geese
on their northern journey home
call to you. Their long

undulant threads pass
in and out of shrouds above
Flown-From-Afar Peak.

Who knows when Mingcheng
will return to touch your cheek?
You miss his caress

more than moonlight. Now,
you've lost the fan he gave you—
one more cause for tears.

ii
WINTER

Tonight as it gets cold
tell yourself
what you know which is nothing
but the tune your bones play
as you keep going. And you will be able
for once to lie down under the small fire
of winter stars.

FROM "LINES FOR WINTER," BY MARK STRAND:

Breath

Frost on the glass—breathe in
open to the glass world. It
breathes back
to prove neither it
nor you can end
this exchange of breath
for worlds.

TESS GALLAGHER

Winter Solstice, Cormorants Roosting

How sleek they are, folding and unfolding
the great scimitars of their wings,
waiting out the bleak December cold
on the spindly balconies of a willow,
its limbs splayed like black lightning
above the pond. It must be well past midnight,
the traffic on Aurora only occasional.

I can just make out the faint rustle
of redwings in the cattails, the plash
of ducks near the shore a pebble-throw
from the park's one bench, the pond stippled
with red ribbons from the nearby Arco sign.
How, hanging in space, do they stay upright
on those twigs the size of pencils?

They resemble urns made of obsidian,
balanced, never toppling, even in wind.
The blue of dawn filters through a row
of alders on the pond's far shore. I recognize
the wheeze of the E-Line bus, making its first run.
They must be chilled on their delicate thrones
on this longest night of the year.

They strike me as pilgrims on a mission
of unknown purpose, weary but dutiful sojourners
hoping to grab a few hours of shut-eye
before a day of diving. I count 79 dark beacons
in the willow. I never believed in angels
until this night. They sleep next to the stars.
They have long curved necks and hooked beaks.

MY NEIGHBOR HOISTS A CONFEDERATE FLAG

To get home, I must drive past his trailer
on the lot next door where the pole stands.
The red-white-blue cloth snaps in wind
or hangs docile, as it does now in the still

summer air. There's some deep failure
where I live, here on Indian lands.
History pretends the country never sinned.
That omission is the bitterest pill

of all, hiding the past from our present selves,
telling stories washed clean by the new owners.
The colors of cruelty scream in his flag.
I want to torch it. I want to toss a can of paint.

My street is where darkness delves—
tents on the church lawn, homeless kids, loners,
enraged whites wearing the name tag
of victimhood. We invaders bear the taint

of crimes against our fellow next-of-kin,
crimes my neighbor's flag celebrates:
centuries of human misery. Why, neighbor? Why?
Your flag stains the wind like a murderous kite.

In sleep, its infected blanket burns my skin.
Whose home *is* this? Whose United States?
Fly your racist flag. My flag is the sky
on a summer day, stars on a winter night.

F-16 FLYBY OVER BRIDAL VEIL FALLS

The trail tunneled through pine and hemlock shade,
hedged by fern, wild rose, islands of salal.
Green hum, branch wince, cone fall – no other sound,
the path blond with dust, needled as it climbed
above water clatter in the ravine.

The air tasted of pine pitch, shade, decay,
smelled of living light, walls of damp basalt.
We could not hear the whisper of the falls,
not yet, only our footfalls on root knots,
the leathery squeak of our boots on stones.

Her ears are keener, sharpened for twig-snap,
birdcall winged from the dark of leaning trees.
She heard the low hum first – a vibration
on snowberry leaves, petals of dogwood.
We both felt a rising rumble. The ground

moved. An end-of-the-world boom, a sound bomb
more hellish than hell's molten hail, dropped us.
Its thunder clung to our skin. The forest,
too, felt it, deafened by the explosion.
Light itself had been wounded, in shock, dazed.

Silence came back from the dead. The faint *shush*
of the creek came back. After the howling,
we did not speak but let the falls tell us
where to climb to feel its wind on our arms
pasted with dust and sweat. Soon, another

version of thunder, not terrifying,
not screams, flames, houses blown to bits; rather,
cymbal and kettle drum delirium
of white fire jetted from a clifftop notch,
funneled to the log-strewn pool where we stood

in braided sunlight and buffets of mist.
We took pictures of flowers and froth where
water crashed into water, churned and foamed.
From the seeth of spray, a rainbow signaled
a lull in the war. We survived. For now.

Valentine's Day 2018
~After Yeats' "Easter 1916"

I've seen them gather at the park,
each with a phone to the ear,
sitting on benches in the near dark
or texting a friend in a friend's car.
I've strolled by, almost old enough
to be great-uncle, reeling back
to their age, to girls' bright laugh,
at boys' crass jokes meant to crack
them up about some foolishness at school—
lighting a joint behind the gym,
doing whatever it took to be cool,
be liked, be someone's chum.
That was then. We endure the Age of Fear.
We call our children our clearest lights,
and to parents that's how they appear.
But not to all, who hold gun rights
dearer than the lives of the young,
they who will skateboard us to the future.
A street-sweeper can be bought for a song.
Thus did they die, student and teacher.
Obligatory thoughts and prayers. It doesn't last.
The Age of Fear has come to stay
like some mental vampire from our past.
They died at school on Valentine's Day.

Oh beautiful for spacious skies…
we'd sing in class. Nice words.
The words turned out to be white lies
we learned by rote. Those herds
of buffalo roaming the prairies?
The new arrivals stole the owners' land
and called it theirs, spun out histories
free of crime. They thought their versions grand.
And guns were part of the grandeur—
to kill buffalo, to hunt down the "savage

tribes" by savage means, to slander
those who lived here, to ravage
and sunder the cultures of a continent.
Here, guns are as countless as stars,
stowed in drawers, closets, a cabinet,
the glove boxes of a million cars.
Prayers didn't protect the Parkland dead.
The Age of Fear blew them away
into storm clouds heavy as lead.
They died at school on Valentine's Day.

And those amber waves of grain,
and the god who shed his grace
on us, entered the American brain
and locked our brains in place.
And the purple mountains majesty,
Disney's Davy Crocket, the Alamo—
fed us a tinted, tainted history.
We didn't know what we didn't know.
Blood spatter patterns cover walls
in the classroom, oh my heart.
Droplets decorate silk ties in the halls
and august chambers of the Senate.
They smear bundles of unmarked bills
those senators gladly accept
to be dead to grief. Their silence kills.
Their silence howls them as corrupt.
Teachers call roll – I do the same
for Teacher Scott; for Nicholas, Martin, Alyssa.
The task at hand is to name each name:
Cara, Gina, Luke, Alaina,
Joaquin, Jamie, Meadow, Carmen.
Among the dead were parents:
Coach Chris, Coach Aaron, Alex, Peter, Helen—
there can never be recompense.
Goodbye to the amber waves.
Goodbye to innocence, that bouquet
of artificial flowers on their graves.
They died at school on Valentine's Day.

Dark Ages

We understood the world then. It had edges, limits. Books were for
the select. We read the weather, studied bones of hens dropped on a
napkin. We read the stars. We knew them as the words of God, each
word an icy iris watching while we slept. We were certain devils lived
in the woods or lurked in a milk pail to lure our maids, or hissed in a
cellar behind the neighbor's barn, or slept in the stomachs of sheep.
The devil's voice lulls, like drops of water falling on a stone.
Love waxed and waned with the moon, or came when snows
burdened our trees, lightened later, washed by the lash of rain,
followed by flowers followed by toil, endless toil. We sheared our
sheep. We endured the pain of our short spans. We understood the
forest was a dark thing, goatish, with a goat's foul breath at night.
We understood mud, decay, the suddenness of fevers, chills, clots of
blood, shrieks as if from a wagon's ungreased wheel. Warnings were
delivered by our Savior, our Heavenly Father who must be stern and
not give in too quickly to our pleas. We were fervent in our ardor
for all things unseen, unverifiable, like the bibles few owned, fewer
still could read. We prayed, of course, often all the long night. God
listened. Trouble was, as like as not, he did little else but glare down,
silent as a barren mountain. Because he did nothing, we prayed all
the more devoutly. Yes, sometimes we were answered. Spring would
arrive – that was proof enough. Fruit trees bore their gifts. Only a few
calves were stillborn. Days were warm and bright. While we tilled
the stony soil, the devil squeezed out of a pig's ass, stood up, put on
his hose, a silk shirt, twisted his cloven hooves inside a pair of fine
leather boots and set off for the next village, his tailored breeches
reeking of manure, his yellow hair smelling of piss.

OKATAR ŠVEC: A BIOPOEM

~ Otakar Švec, sculptor, 1892-1955

How smooth the river was, reflecting trees,
clouds, picnickers along the Vitava bank.
From the hard bench of a tour boat,
even the gothic spires of Prague Castle—
mirrored, inverted – hardly wavered
in the languid current. At night,
he marveled at the flicker of gas lamps
along the Charles Bridge, its statues
of kings and saints glowering over
the flow of history, the flow of humanity
from one shore to another. The bridge had seen
the start and end of wars, empires risen,
empires withered, centuries of foot traffic,
of horse-drawn carts whose wheels grooved
the granite cobbles, polished by bare feet,
feet shod later in leather and sheep skin,
later still in Soviet army-issue boots.
Švec must have crossed the bridge
a dozen times, building in his mind's eye
the colossus that would make him famous.
He pointed to a bluff a quarter mile off.
There, he said to the cool river air. *There*.

He won the contract. His work would tower
a quick tour boat ride downriver from the bridge,
mounted on an immense concrete plinth.
His Stalin, fifty feet from the giant shoes
to the moustache, bushy brows, and swept-back hair,
would stand – a Goliath god – above the river,
his huge face, like the kings and saints
on the bridge, would be both kindly and stern.
Behind the great leader, workers would pose
heroic: one man would wave the party flag,
a young woman would carry the famous sickle.
Perhaps he'd add a priest for good measure.

A Red Army soldier, Švec envisioned,
would stand guard with his rifle, facing backward,
ready to defend the rigid father's forward gaze,
his glorious vision of a bright new dawn.

Five years it took to build his masterwork.
May Day, 1955. The Charles Bridge
blossomed with hanging baskets of flowers.
Geese and strings of goslings glided
in and out of sedges along the Vitava banks.
Bands gathered on every street corner to blare
Soviet anthems as city fathers prepared
for the unveiling, to pull a dozen ropes from tarps
that would reveal the scale of Švec's creation.

Okatar Švec, architect, actor, son of a pastry chef,
had killed himself the night before.
That changed nothing. The unveiling went on.
There's no record of whether citizens
of Prague applauded or merely stood there
on the riverbank or gawked from the bridge
in silent awe at the monstrosity downriver,
the great visage glaring, it seemed, at everything.

Seven years from that spring morning,
it took a ton of explosives to blow up Stalin.
Huge chunks of him sailed into the river.
Prague erupted with parties and music.
For a week, free Pilsner beer flowed freely.

What would divers see on the river bottom?
They might encounter the giant's head,
upturned, eight feet from chin to brow,
half-sunk in silt, eyes blinded by green algae,
glaring still, like the eyes of tyrants of every age.
Maybe they'd see Vitava's famous rainbow trout
nosing about Stalin's ears and shattered jaw,
or weeds woven in the fingers of a severed hand.

Where Okatar Švec lies is anyone's guess.
Perhaps he joined his wife, Vlasta Svecova,
who worked beside him to create a monument
they believed would bring back a mythic lost greatness
and would, like the 600-year-old Charles Bridge,
last for centuries. Vlasta Svecova, too, killed herself
in 1954, a year before the statue's tarps were pulled.

TRAGIC OPERA: RICHARD UND MATHILDA

"Life imitates Art more than Art imitates Life." ~Oscar Wilde

Wagner knew the song of longing, the dread
of never tasting her breasts, she whose keen
mind shut down, a heart no better than dead.
Tristan und Isolde, their heat unsaid, unseen,
they too never touch. No matter how dear,
they cannot do the lovely human deed.
Each wants the other, but they're never near
enough to body forth the living seed.
Wagner well knew the kind of world he drew.
He has the pair doom themselves on a dare.
No potion, no hope, no prayer will undo
a love so taut, so unbearably rare.
Isolde arrives too late. Wounded, Tristan dies.
He's Wagner; she, Mathilda, in thin disguise.

Caning the Raspberries

January chill. The canes have done their work—
dry, hollowed, their brown spears bowed,

most leaves withered, curled into leathery knuckles,
all but a few fallen back to fallow toward spring.

By March, pale shoots will rise from mats
of decay. What it *means* – the upward surge

from earth's dark cellar – I have no more
than a green clue. In a week or two,

as I've done for years, I'll squat and sit.
clippers in hand, to cut back the old dead.

I'll compost the spiny limbs tied with strings of dry
pea vines, thin ropes of runners from pumpkins,

their lanterns extinguished, long gone to soil.
Winter is a comma, a coma broken by upward surge.

Living scaffolds will emerge, pale girders
will leaf out, the first white blossoms will unfurl,

open for the toil of bees – our gold salvation.
Almost overnight, hard nubs will swell,

ripen into blood beads. As I've done for years,
I'll pick the fruit of my labors, rinse off the dust,

mash the mess in a pot, add pectin, sugar,
a cup of water, simmer this ruby mush,

then ladle it into nine jars. Always nine jars.
They will stand at attention on the kitchen

counter to cool and set. In the morning,
I'll move all but one jar to the pantry,

as I've done for years. I'll spread a patch
of jam on toast to taste, to remember the flavor

of winter before dark gave in to light,
light to upward surge, upward surge to blossoms,

blossoms to ripeness, ripeness to sweetness,
sweetness to toast, toast to the point of why

I do what I do, why I bend down at the end of winter
with a pair of rusted clippers and start all over.

Avalanche: A Survival Guide

[Author's note: These instructions have been slightly
modified from a website for backcountry skiers.]

1. *Be a Beacon*
Buried alive. Now, locate your emergency flashlight.
Maybe the search team will see your glow.
Maybe not. Still, think of Jupiter, that white speck,
its moons visible through the mind's binoculars.
Be Jupiter in the night sky. We'll find you, friend,
by your glimmer, that jumble where you're pinned
beneath a shattered mass of rocks, trees and snow.

2. *Stay on Top*
When you hear the crack of doom, when you see
the roiling white fury roaring your way, flatten yourself
like a Jesus surfboard. Catch what may be your last wave.
Ride it out. Be a berserk gymnast to stay above the frayed
seams of our times, an age whose age is finite after all,
its days numbered after all, its towers unstable,
unable to bear the weight of its errors, its white
innocence blasted, thundering down.

3. *Reach for the Sky*
Take it for what it's worth: Clichés, for better or worse,
are sometimes true, as now, reaching for the sky,
you may yet survive by pointing to the blue, flashing
in blips as you tumble. The sky, that teeming sea,
can be a wondrous dream, a vacancy bulging with its own
emptiness. Point to the heart of emptiness.
Claw your way blueward, but – and this is important:
remember to breathe while you gyrate inside the growl
snow makes when it's no longer benign or rational.
Your fingers are broken, bloody, blessedly numb.
Point like there is no tomorrow. Cliché, yes, and true:
there *is* no tomorrow. There *is* no upward or downward.
Never say die. Reach for the sky.

4. *Get Spitting*

We in Search and Rescue could not be more serious.
Being crushed is no laughing matter. Look,
you've been unceremoniously entombed, folded
in a fetal ball, as were your ancestors, eking a living
in a cave, desert, savannah, ice sheet, tundra, plain,
on the bank of a dry streambed, before the first tick of time.
Your spit will form a pocket in the snow compacted
against your face. Do not accept suffocation just yet.
Accept instead the plume of air you've created
with your expectorate. Lower your expectation
that spitting will save you. Then, drink it in, drink deep.
You might just make it back to the world of the so-called
living. You may well find yourself spitting mad at nature.
Save that for later when you rail against the gods
for putting you in harm's way, dropping you as if
you're a web-snared fly, an unfledged quail surrounded
by shotguns in a gun-crazed era. Do you want to live? Spit.

5. *Stay Calm*

If experience is any guide, calm is required both *before*
and after the storm. You've survived, in pain with a fractured
thigh, broken ribs, hammer blows to your head,
still in one piece inside your cracked helmet. Your bruised,
bootless feet may feel warm – a common response to shock,
as any skier who breaks a leg will testify. You're in the dark,
alert but bewildered in the wilderness of the moment.
You're still sensate. If your eyes are not swollen shut,
focus on specks of light. If you see them, they might be real.
Gather your scattered wits in your icy strait-jacket, now
that it no longer feels as if you're wearing a heart attack.
Listen to ice. Its creaks and sighs might suggest you will
never again see the sun. Be at one with this knowledge.
Continue in lighthouse mode. Picture our team at work.
We know you're down there somewhere. We believe
we're close. Believe with us. Be hopeful in a hopeless state.
We're digging our hearts out. Our dogs are pawing, barking.
They've picked up your scent. We have high-tech detectors
too technical to explain here. If there's such a thing as luck,

make it happen. If you make it happen, you'll beat the gods
at their own amusing games. If you beat the odds,
you can tell us your tale back at the ski resort infirmary,
and later retell it to those who love you despite your desire
to ski the steepest runs in the world. You can likewise
report to the world of disbelievers what it felt like
to have caught Death napping. You might even consider
joining our avalanche rescue team, to teach our survival
skills to those who were, like you, unprepared for life
on earth, especially at high elevations among the unseen
forces of chaos. Lessons would include: 1. How to read
a mountain; 2. How to translate the language of snow,
its clicks and chitter; 3. and more generally, How to live
with the unforeseeable nature of everything. One more thing:
most avalanches make no sound. When you hear it,
it's too late. You're inside its gaping maw, whose roar will
deafen you. If we didn't get to you in time, this survival guide
is moot. If we did and you're foolhardy enough to return
to the scene of the crime, follow Steps 1 thru 5, as noted.
Above all, this: Be a beacon. Think of fireflies, glow-worms.
Think of dinoflagellates, those bioluminescent wonders
that cause the surf at night to flare with blue-green fire.
To make it out alive, you may need to give off blue-green fire.

To Step Outside at the End of Winter

is to be greeted by the last mound
of dirty snow just off the porch,

shoveled there some two months past,
is to observe its fringe where the glassed edge

has receded, as if a coverlet has been drawn back,
is to notice purple bleed out of the thawed earth—

a swatch of crocuses clustered together, saying
without saying: the world goes on while you sleep,

goes on and on and will go on being what it is:
a thing like none other in all creation,

and it comes with a nest of velvet thimbles
popped up without fanfare overnight,

requiring no permission, needing nothing but ligh—
is to be, in a glance,

aware of the strange, unaccountable fact
of being alive.

Midnight Midpoint of the Cedar River Bridge

Over the guardrail, some twenty feet down, Chinook salmon—
hundreds, thousands – floated, their spent bodies bluish

under the garish light of sodium lamps. More cars, more semis
than I'd have guessed at that hour. Passing under the bridge,

belly up, drifting sideways, the Chinooks tumbled, luminous,
current-caught, bumping into themselves, already in decay

after their labors to get here, charging past dams, clear-cuts,
factory spills, their silver sides gouged, fins ripped off, tails torn—

all to find Cedar River gravel beds and be, once more, reborn.
Downstream, they will feed bears, minks, eagles, gulls, flies.

Behind my back, traffic roared. The rail hummed in my hands.
Who are they, these drivers? Coming or going? From where

to where? The sidewalk itself trembled. Below: a silent procession.
Up here: a cacophony of cars, headlights, stink of diesel exhaust.

Mad thought: I wanted to block traffic, implore irate drivers
to roll down their windows to hear my lecture on the beauty

of salmon, the perfection of their migration, the precision
of their memory. *Just for two minutes,* I'd say in my calmest voice,

turn off your engines. I swear I'm harmless. Go to the rail.
Look down. Those are the salmon people. Please thank them.

They have been feeding the world for thousands of years. That's it.
Bid them well and return to your cars. The dead are swimming home.

iii
Fall

November always seemed to me the Norway of the year.

Emily Dickinson

DOWNFALL OF THE HALLOWEEN PUMPKIN

I've moved it from the porch to a brick pedestal in the garden.
The bulbous bloated head I'd carved was – at least I thought so—

unnerving: a fiendish grimace with jagged fangs. Neighbor kids
in their Spiderman and Dracula capes, their Wonder Woman

and Bat Girl outfits, would see no orange smiley-face
with twinkling candle-lit eyes on our darkened porch.

Instead, from the top of our drive, they'd catch the flicker
of something ghastly, hellish, a grinning demon on fire.

I wanted them to shudder, to grab the hands
of mom and dad all the tighter before the long walk

with shaky flashlights to our door. For knocking bravely,
they'd be greeted with our shouts of "Happy Halloween!"

Maybe a few kids, still out on the street, would say, "No!
Let's *not* go there!" Maybe a few parents would agree,

would likewise find the orange mouth hideous,
disquieting and – so I hoped – appalling. Crazy? Yes.

I wanted the adults to be struck with horror, to hint that
even in the age of the internet and its conspiracy theories,

semi-literacy the norm, there *is* such a thing as evil.
Now, November, icy rain, brief days of sickly light.

Another killer, the plague, moves about in the guise
of Death swinging his blade. The leering head in the garden

is oblivious. Its face has collapsed, toothless now that squirrels
have bitten off the fangs, chewed the eye sockets wider still,

not unlike a skull's. The stemmed lid has fallen into the shell.
Gray mold trickles from the corner of its mouth, now withered,

no longer able to snarl. Give it a few more weeks.
Let it decompose to mush on its throne of broken bricks.

Let the ghastly image I sculpted when I stabbed the soft flesh
return to earth. Let the orange monster feed the worms.

Holding the Day-Old Baby, I Feel the Feather Weight of My Death

He has arrived earlier than expected,
light as a small bag of windfall apples
in my lap. Now and then he rouses
to blink the black opals of his eyes,
still mostly sightless after all that time
in the dark. I'm his father's father and—
oh, what the hell – I'm on a short leash,
wondering if my departure will likewise
be earlier than expected – which is,
I suppose, always the case. The future
announces itself as a quiet, insistent
tap at the door. The new being
in the crook of my arm yawns.
Now his lips part in a reflexive dream-smile
I take to mean he finds the condition
of being alive curious, wryly amusing,
as if to say, *So, where am I exactly?*
on this bright November morning,
a day I've already subtracted
from the dwindling total. His eyelids flutter,
thinner than the skin of a hatchling robin.
Now I'm reminded babies must eat.
His mother whisks him out of my arms,
off to a rocker in a dark corner,
where, after a few urgent squalls, he's quiet,
the sucking loud even from across
the room. I'm empty-handed once more,
happy in a way I've never been.
I plan to attend his third birthday,
already scripting, after the other kids
have left with their frosting-smeared chins,
the conversation we might have,
the one where I tell him I held him
when he was one day old, his eyes
were exquisite blueberries, different
than the gray-green they are now.

He'll be only mildly impressed,
more interested instead in tearing off
the paper of one last gift:
a box with a silver latch and key.
He's wide-eyed to lift the wooden lid,
to get a glimpse of things to come.
I'm more intrigued in learning how
to tie together strings of time,
quilting swatches of months and years,
stitching my life to his, as if I had such power,
the slightest ability to forestall for even
an instant that insistent tap
from arriving sooner than expected.
Still, I'm swaddled in the glory
of the moment, thankful to have held him,
to listen to his mother hum in the dark,
to hear the creak of the rocker
on the hardwood floor.

~Cosmo MacKenzie Harkness, b. November 5, 2019

Italian Prune

Wounded, scarred, the tree's been dying for years.
Sap has oozed into glass nodes the color
of whiskey, limbs lichen-sleeved – tufts robins
yank at nesting time. Each March, buds unfold

into ovate leaves. Last year's prune harvest
was sparse – less than a dozen hard green nubs
swelled into dusky purple eggs. Squirrels
made off with them in a single morning.

I've thought to cut it down. I'm not sure why
I haven't done so. That's me all over:
sure and unsure, depending on the month.
My ladder stands near as tall as the tree.

Uncertain how to grow despite its age,
its arthritic trunk is the size of my calf.
Ten minutes, my limb saw would bring it down.
I'd do it now if it weren't for the spiked

white blossoms that will appear overnight
come mid-April, more startling than spring snow,
their fragrance almost too faint to detect—
an imagined tang, like honey-sweetened

lemonade in a glass across the room.
I can't count the times I've stood here,
saw in gloved hand, ready to do the deed,
then walked back to the tool shed, hung the saw

on its nail and called it a day. This day,
November's bitter chill has settled in.
Most leaves have dropped, strewn like potato skins.
I might have retraced my steps to the shed

but for a patch of afternoon sunlight
in an upper branch, catching a spider
hard at it, knotting one strand of its net
to the next with its eight knitting needles.

Unspooled from the spider's brown spinneret,
strands gleam, prismatic, iridescent,
as if the tiny pouch contained a star.
I might have cut this tree five years ago,

or last fall, or now, in the failing light.
That would mean the end of sweetness. There'd be
no prunes to savor (if saved from squirrels).
Instead of the tree, or the orb spider's

electric wire that draws my jaded eye,
I suppose I'd be gazing absently
at power lines, crows on their way to roost,
or, drooped on a pole in my neighbor's yard,

the limp cloth of an American flag.
If not for the fruit, then for the silver
thread the spider pulls from itself, for spiked
blossoms sure to come, for what vanishes,

what remains, for a tree that perseveres
in ill-health, for those I forgive, those who
forgive me, for the irreplaceable
world entire, the saw will stay on its nail.

Coyolxauhqui's Stone
~Templo Mayor Museum, Mexico City

No one pays much attention this morning
to the headless goddess,
her limbs hacked off, the dismembered pieces
etched in a great round stone.

Construction crews back-hoed the mythic stone,
buried six hundred years
deep in Aztec earth, heart of the empire.
Here stood *Templo Major*,

its twin pyramids a blaze of white fire.
Coyolxauhqui[1], she whose
cheeks have bells, whose light enchants the night air,
had four hundred brothers.

One, Huitzilopochtli[2], was born feathered,
a hummingbird in full
armor. He kills his sister for her plot
to slaughter their mother.

It's a long, twisted story, like our times.
He chops sister up, throws
her bloody parts down the steep temple stairs.
Someone – we don't know who—

picks up her head and flings it to the sky
where she becomes the moon.
Strollers ignore Coyolxuahqui's body,
entranced by the new god,

Smart Phone, oblivious of the huge stone
nearby, the severed arms
and legs of the goddess sculpted to last.
Blind as well to the bells

on her cheeks, her feathered headdress, a skull
tied to a belt of snakes
about her waist. They blow off the moonlight
she casts across the world,

draping great skyscrapers and cathedrals
of Tenochtitlan[3]
– Mexico City. Over time, horror
can become luminous,

radiant, like Coyolxauhqui,
butchered by a brother
for reasons so obscure they don't make sense.
We believe what we're told.

History swims with corpses, sacrificed
on this altar or that,
hearts cut out to appease this god or that.
Coyolxauhqui shines. Hers

is a long, twisted story, like our times.
Moonlight gets the last laugh.
Her four hundred brothers, the stars, flare far
behind her lustrous head.

[1]*coy-yol-zah-key*

[2]*weet-see-luh-powch-tuh-lee*

[3]*teh-know-sheet-lan*

AT THE CURLING RINK

I can no longer feel my feet. Even at 13, in my thin-soled sneakers,
  the world wore an ominous grin. Here, in this weird bowling alley,
was a case in point. My father – still in his polished work shoes,

  necktie tucked into his shirt, the flaps of his orange, fur-line hat
pulled down – crouches over the granite stone. His gloved hand
  grips the handle, one knee on the ice, his head bowed as if lost

in a prayer of contrition. He glances up, left and right, at his teammates
  ready with their brooms. They nod. He pushes himself forward,
the stone moving with him just below his chin. He releases the stone

  as if ejecting in slow motion some heavy part of himself. *Sweep!*
calls the captain to the sweepers. They scoot sideways with the creaking
  slide of the stone, smacking the ice like a demented clean-up crew.

At the time, I could not fathom why my father and the men—
  who rarely talked – were utterly absorbed in a sport in which
almost nothing happens. Still, it was hypnotic. I knew then my role

  in life would be to take note, to observe. I'd need to come up with a plan
to appear normal, to go on living in this icy theatre of the absurd,
  in the glare of the rink neon, my toes frozen, while heavy round stones

float dream-like toward the colored rings of the target.
  Shuffleboard was thrilling by comparison. I still see
the smoke of my father's breath clouded above him,

  still hear the *slap-slap* of the brooms on the ice, the captain shouting
Sweep! or *Halt!* followed by the *clack* of colliding stones.
  Once, under winter stars, walking back to the car, his gloved hand

in my gloved hand, I asked, Who won? They did, he said.
  Has our team ever won? He smiled, looked at me and said nothing.
Then: How about we, just the two of us, go grab a burger and a shake.

41

MY FATHER'S UNCLES DOING TIME

Their sorry, sorry asses. Bad year, 1929.
Neither one is yet 30 in the grim prison photos
I received from the state archives.
Dull-eyed, sullen – greasy dark hair on one,
fair strands drape the forehead of the other,
both faces aged and lined from the morphine
they couldn't get out of their systems.
Bad year, 1917, the Great War winding down,
but not the "soldier's disease,"
nor the Spanish Flu pandemic to follow.
Fifty million swept off across
the sorry, sorry earth. Bad year, 1918.
Their mother wrote to the governor—
her penciled words will bring tears
to your eyes, as they did the governor's.
Sir, she said, *my boys are sick. Prison
will kill them first, and I will follow.
Sir, I'm on my knees.* He signed the pardons
and they walked. Too late. They were yo-yos,
in and out and in, addle-brained by dope.
One taught himself leathercraft inside:
studded belts, purses, holsters—
tooled with acorns, oak leaves, roses
you can smell. On the billfold
in my back pocket is the carved head
of a horse so fine you want to reach out,
let it bat its eyes and nuzzle your hand.
Morphine and time did its work on them.
Dad once took me to a hospital where
Sweetie – that was his name, Sweetie,
younger of the two – lay dying. Gray faced,
eyes hollowed, he turned to me, smiled,
did not or could not speak. Somehow,
there on his bed, he managed to lift one hand.
I still feel his cool fingers on my wrist.

I'd never seen needle tracks. There they were,
mapped along his splotchy arms.
Seeing Sweetie that day, I learned a lesson
about cruelty, how it peers over the top of a trench,
waits for you across the cratered expanse
of no-man's land, takes aim and fires,
not to kill, but to disfigure, maim.
You're never the same. You find ways
to hide the scars. It's a losing proposition.
I grieve for their sorry, sorry asses.
for the sickness that befell them,
for the wounds that left them lame
all the days of their sorry, sorry lives.

My Father Meets Margaret Bourke-White

The encounter happens aboard a troop ship crossing the Atlantic.
He has just turned nineteen, a newly trained B-17 gunner.

She is twice his age, a photographer for *Life* magazine, striking
in her leather flight jacket when they meet on deck one clear night,

the moon low, its blue road undulant in the ship's wake.
Good evening, young man, she says. *Cigarette?*

He has seen her in newsreels. He's flustered, near speechless.
I don't smoke, ma'am. She pulls out a pack of Camels.

Your first crossing, I gather. Salt air stings his nose.
I'm from Bremerton, he tells her, as if she has asked.

She looks out into the dark. *Well, prepare yourself,
my young friend from Bremerton. I'm told the Gulf of Naples*

*is on fire from oil, full of sunken ships, half the buildings leveled.
We'll see for ourselves soon enough. So, buona fortuna.*

Benvenuto in Italia. He studies the glow of her cigarette.
She is taller than he by inches. *How'd the world get this way?*

she says, not so much to him but to a maze of stars. They lean
on the rail, her arm against his in its tan GI-issue sleeve.

We'll see Gibraltar at dawn, she says. *Portside.* Moonlight
silvers her hair. He finds a Hershey bar in his breast pocket,

breaks off half, offers it to her. She flicks her cigarette overboard,
takes the chocolate. *Thanks, kiddo.* Later, she will show the world

skeletal survivors of Buchenwald, the mushroom cloud
over Nagasaki, Gandhi at his spinning wheel, anti-apartheid protestors

near Johannesburg facing whips and guns of Afrikaner police.
Now, she stands by my father, neither one prepared for what

awaits them, neither one aware that this night will become
a war souvenir, one he will, toward the end of his life,

share with me, vivid as the glass green Adriatic he'd cross
on dozens of missions from his airbase in Foggia,

intense as the time he knew he'd die, his bomber lost in fog
over the Alps. *Climb!* he shouts into his intercom to the pilot.

I can see snow, rocks! I see the tops of trees! Crammed inside
his plexiglass ball in the plane's belly, his task is to count

the nine five-hundred-pounders released from the bay doors,
track them as they tumble dream-like toward Vienna, Hamburg,

Cologne, Berlin. Five miles down, people die, he understands,
inside houses and building, in parks and on street corners. They die

in tiny puffs of smoke opening like gray roses. He'd recall that night
with Bourke-White, the silver of her hair, sharing his chocolate bar

on the portside deck. Leaning together on the railing at sunrise,
their arms still touching, the Rock of Gibraltar rises before them,

cathedral-like, washed in gold. *Beautiful* he says. *Yes*, she says.
Remember it, my young friend. In two days we land in Naples.

My Mother's Underpants

My mother's threadbare underpants fall off while she browses
women's clothing in an upscale department store.

Do the gods witness these things? A well-coifed clerk witnesses it.
Mom has asked about the price of a skirt, or the size, or the color.

I'm two months old. I snooze through this minor disaster in my stroller,
blinking at the glittery skin of the ceiling, irritated by the smell

of perfume, not having any words yet, like *perfume* or *underpants* or *gods*.
The clerk studiously avoids glancing down. She knows.

My mother knows. The underpants around her ankles are gray, the fabric
torn in places, the elastic band having lost its muscle tone.

The two women stand there among cashmere sweaters, rayon blouses,
near the aisle of the latest purses from Italy, near the shoe department

we just passed through, with its cordovan brown calf-high lace-up boots
from Paris – items my mother cannot imagine buying.

This afternoon she wears canvas flats, their thin soles worn through.
Even with nylon socks, she feels the cool department store linoleum.

It's like stepping on dimes. I'm in a wet diaper. My brain
is the size of a peeled orange, so I'm unaware of much beyond

the sway of my stroller, the pleasing bumps of its wheels
on the rising and falling escalator stairs, the coming-and-going smell

of my mother, the chirps of her voice. It's not clear if the clerk
fully understand the panic of the young woman before her.

What she does see is my mother's brown coat, missing its top button.
I'm rather busy at the moment with another customer, the clerk says.

Is there anything I can help you with? My mother wants to whisper
No, thank you, but the best she can do is nod her head, then corrects

herself and shake her head. Sometime after my 15th birthday
my mother will tell me the story of her fallen underpants.

We laugh about it. It's funny, like those small injuries we suffer,
the not-quite-trivial humiliations that expose us to ourselves.

Time softens them. Some – those hidden stories of our lives—
we bury deep. Did it really happen? Yes, it really happened.

The gods do witness these things. Sometimes they laugh, as we do.
Is this the "divine comedy," one asks, I've heard about?

More often than not, they shrug, turn to one another and say,
The poor woman's pants fell off. I thought I'd seen everything.

"Brown Eyes"

Under the silver grinder by the shelf of day-old bread,
he'd crawl on all fours to find coffee beans while his mother shopped.

He'd sweep them up with his palm, crouch behind the apple bin,
and put in his mouth one bean at a time. He'd suck on them a while,

then chew, eager for the strange acids to leap inside his eyes.
He'd sneak into a corner and spit out the bitter grains.

Mother knocked on the cantaloupes. Then, once, Bud, the butcher,
slender curved knife in his hand, looked down and said,

"Well, young man. How about a song?" "He's shy,"
said his mother. "Honey, sing 'Brown Eyes' for Mr. D'Angelo."

The boy swallowed the handful of beans under his tongue,
turned away to face the shelves of Campbell's Soup and sang—

whispered, rather – pushing out with all his might the words
to the old tune: *Beautiful, beautiful brown eyes. I'll never love*

blue eyes again. Years later, that moment would return.
He would taste them still, those bitter beans from the floor,

still taste the words to the song as they had risen
from his thin chest. He would see himself in the aisle

among bags of flour, stacked boxes of bottled Dr. Pepper,
near trays of bloody steaks, chickens, slabs of bacon,

their smells dizzying in the warmth of a summer afternoon.
Once again, the words would catch in his throat. His heart

would thump just as it had then. He wondered if anyone—
besides himself – might come to see the act of a child

singing to a man in an apron smeared with blood
as a kind of bitterness, something never quite swallowed,

still hidden under the tongue, chewed in secret. Bitter
they were, those beans, always bitter, always delicious.

TELLING TAURUS HOW IT IS

If the Bull has ever been brighter—
the head straight ahead, arrowhead-like,
not yet fallen below the toothed silhouette
of Clemens Ridge – I don't know when.
Through aspens, the river drones an endless *hush*.

Bright friend, we've mastered the new lingo,
our speech muffled, masked: *quarantining,
social distancing*. We eat our daily bread
of uncertainty, worried sick by the new sickness,
passed to us by innocent others,

passed by us to innocent others.
I think of the plague closing the theatres
in London, of Shakespeare turning
from plays to that more inward form,
the sonnet, a shift from public to private

ways of saying what our lives mean.
Tonight, I wish to speak to your five stars as,
one by one, they disappear
behind the ridgeline, more beautiful
now that they're gone.

I want to tell them what it was like,
what we loved, why we kissed and hugged
each other, or got into arguments
or hurt people we didn't even know
or did know but hurt even so.

I want to tell your five stars
how on a dare we'd leap into a frigid
alpine lake or marvel at lichens
on basalt walls or study photos of our kin—
unsmiling, long dead – in old albums.

Certain as a moonless night, we must suffer
what we must suffer. We'll kiss again one day
or pat each other on the shoulder or hold
a lover's hand on Clemens Ridge, awed once more
by grains of light scattered across the night sky.

Deux Rondeaux

1.
More and more I repeat myself. Even this
note to swallows, alders, summer and fall
echoes again off the canyon wall.

Each time we kiss, love, it's the first kiss.
The others? Gone. Some I well recall.
More and more I repeated myself. Even this
note to sparrows, willows, summer and fall.

Years drop from calendars into the abyss,
Word by word: names, places, birdsong…all.
But then…a vase of roses in the hall.
More and more I repeat myself. Even this
note to winter, spring, summer and fall
echoes again off the canyon wall.

2.
Two petals appeared this morning, one red,
one yellow, fallen from the Ball jar vase.
We're brief as breath, like grief, like grace.

We're comets at twilight, you said.
We're twin stars, face to aging face.
This evening I count five, love, three red,
two yellow, fallen from the Ball jar vase.

The permanent parting – that's what I dread,
not being here or anywhere, lost in space.
When roses wilt, a scent lingers in their place.
This morning, a scattering: five red,
four yellow, fallen from the Ball jar vase.
We're brief as breath, like grief, like grace.

iv
SUMMER

Hot town, summer in the city
Back of my neck getting dirty and gritty
Been down, isn't it a pity?
Doesn't seem to be a shadow in the city
All around, people looking half dead
Walking on the sidewalk, hotter than a match head

"SUMMER IN THE CITY," LYRICS BY JOHN SEBASTIAN

Oradour-sur-Glane: A Guided Tour
~*France, June 10, 1944*

Stop 1 – The Church:
German officers faked a reason to cordon off the town.
The small church you see proved useful, now shuttered to all

but the occasional curious tourists like us, its tawny bricks
laid six hundred years ago, its interior blackened.

Flakes of shattered stained-glass glitter still, swept in piles
near the altar, before a statue of Jesus looking up from his cross

as if to say *But...why?* German bullets pock the unrepaired walls.
Blood still darkens the mortar between marble tiles.

Stop 2 – First Café:
Here's where people sat spring days, sipped coffee in tiny cups
to read last week's *Le Monde* or whisper the latest names

of local men and boys listed as dead or MIA.
Who, they'd ask each other, will tend the vineyards

across the creek? Who will harvest the grapes if not the vanished
men and boys? I heard this very morning on the wireless,

someone says, about a big event underway in Normandy.
Très grand et terrible. Les anglais, les américains.

Stop 3 – Bike Shop
These are the remains. It looks just as it did after the fires
died out. A rusted tandem frame, like a sculptor's idea

of an abstract Christ, hangs in twisted agony on a charred
brick wall, one of a few that withstood the flames.

Stop 4 – The Square:
Soldiers ordered townsfolks from their homes
onto the placid grass of the square, men led off

in groups of ten, women and the young marched
along the stream's willow-shaded path to the church,

told no harm would come if they'd calm their children,
or use a hand to stop their whimpering mouths.

Stop 5 – Debris:
Here's the charred skeleton of a pram in a fenced-off
heap of rubble. Here's the body of a treadle-driven

Singer sewing machine, its painted name visible,
half-buried in bricks, just as it was found.

Stop 6 – Second Café:
Here's the ribcage of a café table, same kind
you'd find today along the Seine in far-off Paris,

table just the size for a pair of lovers
to talk about a movie or book or wedding date.

Stop 7 – Auto Repair Shop:
an auto repair garage, roofless now. The car's grill snarls
a gape-toothed grinning skull. Someone in the village

a gape-toothed grinning skull. Someone in the village
parked it here and never drove it again. I imagine it

new, *circa* 1930s, bought when no one in far-off Paris
dreamed of war. Best guess: a Mercedes,

German, made before the war, before the world
became inhuman, before German soldiers scaled ladders,

knocked out with their rifle butts windows, fitted
and glazed in the Middles Ages, and opened fire.

Stop 8 – The Dead:
To remember the dead of Oradour-sur-Glane, you must
imagine the sound of bickering at a vegetable stand,

the nicker of horses in a stable, the fevered voice of Piaf
quavering from a Victrola in the town's one *boulangerie*.

You must reconstitute from dust the 642 who lived here.
You must revive a scene of children at play on the cobbles,

while others run across an open field, twilight settling
like a comforter. You must hear the shout of a girl

to her friends, *Je le vois!* – I see it! – when,
flat on her back on that night in June, the sun's afterglow

smeared on the brow of a hill, she spies Venus,
the evening star. *Ma fleur,* she calls to it. *Ma petite fleur*.

In the High Sierra

In the thin Sierra air, after 10 rutted jeep track miles
above Tahoe, near tree-line, the scent of pine pitch

heavy in August heat, Uncle Charles believes he's found
a certain section of a certain creek where we will fish

for lunker cutthroats my cousin Will says are big as our forearms.
Maybe we'll find browns or goldens hungry for our lures,

the flash of silver in pools where blue turns black.
I've never fished. My casts immediately snag in willows

drooped above a pool. Will's the pro. His line keens from the reel
to the precise point where the eddy curls like a cat asleep,

cat of all colors – rock shade, leaf green, sun-patch, one
prism-edged cloud. Life is pointless. I'm snarled, pole half-mooned,

my tugs futile till the twig snaps, the silver spinner bullets my way.
I shield my eyes. The hook embeds in the pad of my thumb,

barb protruding. I want to yelp. I will not yelp. I'm fifteen.
I yank. The hook comes away with a red morsel of my flesh.

Will pushes aside the willow drapery to ask Any bites?
The look on his face when he sees my thumb. The look.

He can't know in three years he will find himself in Quang Tin
Province, a helicopter mechanic. That's gotta hurt, he says.

I forget the pain. We're on the patio of heaven. He peels
a bandage he found in his tackle box. Blood drips on my bare knee,

on my white shorts, in the creek's wavy glass. He can't know
he has three years and odd months to live. Only I know that.

I know it without knowing it. Near midnight, three plus years
from now, the phone will ring. I'm the one who will take the call.

Pelicans Diving

They skim so close to waves
they must themselves be waves.
Their wingtips kiss the swells.
Then they climb, arm muscles
synced with shoulder muscles
sheathed in flight feathers back-
drafted to lift them high
enough to plumb their own
reflections. It's the gift
of penetrating sight:
to catch the glint of skin,
a sudden seething school.
From that height, they hover
for a heartbeat, no more.
The cudgels of their bills
aimed, wings drawn sleek, they dive
angled like incoming
missiles to shatter
the placid blue window
of warped glass. A plume sprays
up, their prey stunned and scooped.
The world's a carnivore.
You might not imagine
so, seeing pelicans
at rest dockside, afloat
offshore or on postcards,
where they have the comic
look of balding scholars.
The hunger for beauty's
glittering skin requires
blasting through surfaces
with force, snatching the wild
living prize of the hunt,
then to assume a state
of Zen-like quietude,
as if life and death are
two separate species,

different as sea and sky.
There's a ferocity
in the art of nature,
an illusory calm
in the nature of art.
When they glide, pelicans
are all effortless grace,
untouched by gravity
above the curled white crests.
When they plunge to capture
what they need, the silly
scholars become killers.

THE POETICS OF LEONARD

~But the greatest thing by far is to have a command of metaphor.
This alone cannot be imparted by another; it is the mark of genius,
for to make good metaphors implies an eye for resemblances.
Aristotle, from *The Poetics*, S.H. Butcher, trans.

He did not say I have to relieve myself, nor did he say I have to urinate
or I have to take a leak, or the simple, direct I gotta pee. None of that.

He did not say the tiresome Nature calls. What he said was, after we'd
loaded our chainsaws, gas cans, axes, wedges, mauls and lunch pails

in the back of his rattletrap Ford pickup, with its mirrorless side mirror,
its bald tires, after we'd covered our load of cord wood – split rounds

of slash-pile tamarack and red fir left after a recent cutting on a stripped
hillside above Rattlesnake Creek – saws and wood now draped by an oil-rank

tarp, after we sat in the shade of a lone elderberry tree on that chewed-up
patch of earth dented with cat tracks, littered with crushed seedlings,

mangled stalks of wild rose, after we tossed back two cans of warm beer
found by some miracle behind the cab seats, neither of us uttering a word

all that time, aware of no other sound but the shush of a creek downslope
in a thicket of aspens, after surveying the slash-pile – thin, unusable logs

strewn like a tangle of chopsticks, after wiping sweat and sawdust
from our faces with a ratty towel pulled from the glove box, after we gazed

for a time at the odd uplift of distant Meek's Table, tipped for all the world
like the risen bow of the Titanic, its aft slipping beneath a green sea

of ponderosa pine, Leonard turned his dust-washed face to me where we sat.
Flecks of saw wood stuck to his white whiskers, his brow sun-reddened,

the sparse hairs on his head sweat-smeared – at which point he said in his clear, operatic tenor: Well, my good man, I'm gonna drain my lily. He rose

and wandered off. What we talked about on the spine-crunching drive down the curves of Bethel Ridge Road, I couldn't say. I recall the rank smell

of saw oil, the perfume of fresh-cut wood, and Leonard's face asquint, patched with elderberry shade, declaiming as if on stage, I'm gonna drain my lily.

Unable to Waken

And the echoes began
their wings broken
and glaciers wept themselves to sleep
their towers fallen

their wings broken
and the seasons unraveled
their towers fallen
and the seas rose higher

and the seasons unraveled
their webs no longer woven
and the seas rose higher
their currents misguided

their webs no longer woven
and the songbirds migrated toward silence
their currents misguided
and their forests flared all summer

and the songbirds migrated toward silence
their routes disrupted
and their forests flared all summer
their biographies unwritten

their routes disrupted
and rivers wandered the desert
their biographies unwritten
and starlight appeared in daylight

and rivers wandered the desert
their salmon lost in the ocean
and stars appeared in daylight
their warnings disregarded

their salmon lost in the ocean
and glaciers wept themselves to sleep
their warnings disregarded
and the echoes began

The Last Time

It happened on the pier, your back against a railing, masts of several sloops
to your right, topped with their colored flags, the sea behind and to your left—

a warped sheet of tin. As proof it really happened, your friend took a picture
just before I stepped forward toward your opened arms, my face mirrored

in your snazzy sunglasses, your hair in long silver braids – as if such proof
would reveal the moment before the moment the world changed.

We were never lovers, lovers only in the sense of love for those scalable,
sometimes reachable, imagined summits we ascend in the silent odd hours.

That step toward your arms meant we were old friends, heart friends.
I introduced you to my true love, who hugged you, and to my son, who,

with baby in a chest-carrier, hugged you. Steam, I recall, rose from planks
laid out, you'd mentioned, during the pandemic of 1918, the tar softened,

sun-warmed after a morning squall. A man chomping a cigar stub walked by,
pushing a wheelbarrow of oysters. His red rubber boots glistened. In *our* plague,

to save each other, we mask ourselves, we do not hug. That distant moment
marked the last time, on that pier, your face in full sun, your back against a railing.

GUN CULTURE

Thunder kills the silence of the woods. We freeze,
as when on TV or in real life a cop, pointing a gun,
shouts "Freeze!" Which is what we're doing in this instance,
reminded once again: We're at war. This is the front line.

It's summer in the mountains, we're in shorts so we must
watch out for the sting of nettles on our secret narrow path,
a steep one, you often have to guess where to step—
this root or that rock. We've set out to find the bottom of the gorge,

from there to gaze back up in wonder how it was we did not fall.
We've come to face a wall across the creek, basalt columns
arrayed in pure verticality, architected across eons of uplift,
some two hundred sheer feet of dark stone. But now,

gunshots, one echoing report, another, a third. I don't recall
if I shrieked. I may have merely gasped and held my breath.
She, my life guide, uttered not a sound. As if shot herself,
she dove in a thicket of wild rose, shaped herself into a ball.

She's scratched. Specks of blood dot the length of her thigh.
The shooters are close, invisible, really fucking close. So here
we are, having bushwhacked, skidding on loose gravel,
to see the *Thunderbird*, our private name for the rock form rising,

the columns here in wavy symmetry, fanned in a pattern impossible
not to imagine as tail feathers on the lower half, flared wings higher.
Higher still, something like a great crested head turns to the side.
The creek has undercut the wall to perfect the illusion of a stone bird

god hovering in the air above a pool as if weightless, just alighting.
We'd failed to hear the jeep. Now we see it in what looks to be
a hunter's clearing, half-hidden behind a screen of aspens, its huge
wheels muddied, a tattered Confederate flag attached to the antenna.

How they managed to crash through the brush to get here
we could not fathom. Surely there's the remnant of a logging road
somewhere near, one we had not seen. The *shush* of water
slapping stones must have muffled the grind of their engine.

Wind in the pines might have dampened the anger of their tires.
Or they'd been there all along, the two young men, both bearded,
necks and arms tattooed. One has marked his face with olive drab camo.
We see them, they us. My guide still cowers in the thicket. Guys turn

to fire more rounds from their huge black handguns, aimed
at the *Thunderbird*, the shots booming. Puffs of rock dust
fly from the wings. *Guys! Hold your fire. We're leaving.*
My guide shouts *Please stop!* so loud it hurts my ears.

The one with the marked-up face, his khaki shirt emblazoned
with *Semper Fi*, strolls over. He does not glance down
at my guide, still crouched in the thorns of a wild rose,
whose small pink flowers have a smell so sweet and intense

you never forget it. And it strikes me now – that weird mingling
of the odor of roses and the foul acridity of burnt gunpowder.
Guy never looks at her, only at me. *So what's her problem?*
he says. I still hear him: "So what's her problem?"

I must have mumbled something about us being frightened
by shooting, to which he says they'd quit firing
for a few minutes if we chose to leave. *Your call*, he says.
Still hear that too: "Your call." Still see specks of blood

on my guide's arm on the hike out, up the thorny path
not-a-path to the canyon top. Still see her daub the specks
with a tissue. Pale, shaken, she said not one word the entire
way to our car. If I spoke, it would have been in my head,

that thing I always do – replay the scene over and over,
wishing I'd shouted *Hey, motherfucker. How about we stay.*
How about you and your neo-Nazi bro' climb back in the jeep
and jerk off somewhere else! I wanted to tell them,

for all the good it would do, to take their fucking guns and go
fuck themselves. I'd never have said it. They had guns.
Besides, I still argue with myself, what's the point?
How could I explain the majesty of those basalt radials

patched with orange lichens, or ask them to take note of those
nameless blue flowers clinging impossibly to the sheer walls,
lodged in the seams of the slate gray columns. See there, I'd say.
Squint a little. You can make out the wide stone wings, right?

It's a natural wonder, no? Why shoot a bird god sent to us
from the sky? Help me understand your mind. That day,
I didn't tell the bearded men what they could do with their guns.
I've waited till now, for all the good it will do, to explain.

Floaters

Myodesopsia, she says, would be
the technical term. At your age,
she adds, not at all uncommon.

Her jacket is white. Silver hoop earrings.
Her own eyes are kind, sea green.
She's younger than your youngest son.

You see those cobwebs often—
hair-like filaments of lint
suspended in the aged vitreous,

a perpetual twilight you're only
half aware has fallen over the world.
Like vague comets,

they tinge your visions.
These dark threads worm across your eyes
when you swim the backstroke

on summer's final afternoons.
You roll over from the crawl,
push your goggles up to your brow

and float, borne on the lake's
cool quilt to face a few wisps of clouds,
the blue forever, the blades of your arms

swung back to grab water,
to pull yourself through it,
the blue forever obscured

by swimming bits of debris
gathered over a lifetime of seeing.
Myodesopsia. Floaters.

Halfway across the lake, on your back,
you make out at the edges of sight
the filaments of swallows,

a dozen or so, hard to count—
a flock of tiny scissors, so high,
so fuzzy, you can't say for sure

they're swallows or floaters.
Not uncommon at your age,
she said. There, on cruise control,

slapping the lake, your heart hot
with the rhythm of kicks and strokes,
your hands throw up handfuls of jewels.

There, adrift in the late late-middle
of your life, you choose to believe
—all evidence to the contrary—

those dancing threads you see
are not floaters at all. They're swallows,
alive, suspended in the blue forever.

PHEASANTS

Did a shed stand here? The grass tall and blond?
As a kid, he'd been
beauty-struck by the blood-red wattles, plumed
tail feathers – their sheen
in morning sun. He'd crouch beside the shed,
waiting for the grass
to quiver, waiting for them to appear
in the near clearing,
the brazen male, the subtler female,
three bronze chicks behind.

The toolshed is history. A townhouse
with three-car garage
is history's revision. Tall blond grass lies
beneath the asphalt
of a tennis court. He saw pheasants here.
How stately they were—
how struck he was to hear the male's forlorn
calls, like sobs choked back.

He remembers how long he'd gaze, waiting
to be beauty-struck.
Shadowed shed with the hinged door, windows gone,
its roof half-collapsed,
full of old tools not much used anymore:
whipsaw, froe, adze, scythe—
gone to rust. Despite deafness, failing sight,
he hopes even so
to be beauty-struck. He'll never again
be 12. Even so,
he knows the tall blond grass is gone for good,
the pheasants with it.
A shed stood here where
he would crouch, waiting for them to appear,
to strut, to catch fire.

KITE, KALALOCH BEACH

My job: to hold her kite, the blue one
with a snapping yellow tail, the twine taut,
tugging like a fair-sized cutthroat. Her job:
to sprint around in her underwear on the beach

aglow in late summer light. Come see
my jelly fish, Poppy, she yells. Hurry!
I lash the twine to a piece of driftwood.
There's the jellyfish, a glassy blob on the sand.

Will it hurt if I touch it? No, no. It won't hurt
if you touch it. Poppy, where's my kite?
I turn to see it sail away, a crazed shirt flailing,
well beyond breakers full of the sun's late fire.

For some minutes we watch the kite drift—
a scrap of tissue in the deepening blue, the yellow tail
visible until there's nothing to see but the long blade
of the horizon. We listen to waves collapse,

clapping the sand. *Eternity*, I say, mostly to myself.
Poppy, is my kite gone? Yes. It's gone. Poppy,
what's eternity? Her sea-green eyes are urgent.
The best I can do is point to the end of the sky.

V

FUTURE SPRING

I wake from dreams.
Why must unhappy people
                              still get up?

White morning dew drips
from the flowering T'ung trees
                              in the garden.
An idle ramble
          was my new-spring thought.

Will the sun go high
          and scatter mists?
Shall I look?
Will the day be clear,
                    or not?

LI QINGZHAO, 1084-1155

DIY: A Step-By-Step Guide to Jump-Start that Poem You Always Meant to Write But Never Did

The poem knocks like a Bible salesman on your brain's front door.
Your first chore is to find the cigar box of a dozen fountain pens

collected over the decades. One worked. The others bled
like amputees in your hand, tattooed forever in your formative teens.

Find the box. Look for the pale green pen. Wash the barrel
in the kitchen sink until the water runs clear. Next, descend

the stairs that lead to the family crypt where generations
of basement spiders have lived happily in lightless corners

among some yet-to-be-classified molds. Hidden in that dungeon
lies buried a Sheaffer Scrip bottle of ink still in its blue and yellow box.

If the gods are kind, if they find themselves amused by your rummaging
among the dust-lacquered suitcases containing only they know what—

if the ink is there at all, it will turn out to be peacock blue. This time,
the gods have smiled. You've found the bottle. Give a silent cheer,

relieved to know you needn't invent paper. Thank the Chinese
for that. Thank Cai Lun, a mid-level government scribe, whose recipe

included mulberry bark, rags, hemp, mashed with water into pulp,
rolled into mushy napkins and hung out to dry. Cai made paper

from soup 2000 years before you scrawled your first crayon scribbles
on your mother's college textbook, *Gardner's Art Through the Ages.*

And because you found the Scrip bottle, you needn't grind
your own ink, as Japanese sumi-e painters do to put themselves

in the right frame to paint bamboo, a bird on a twig, or a character
that resembles an interesting house, 家, and in fact means "house,"

in Chinese, *jiā.* Dip the tip of the pen in the bottle's well,
pull the lever that sucks in ink, squirting it back in the bottle

a few times as a test. Task completed, now seek out that unused
journal, the one long-departed Aunt Madeline gifted you

on your fourteenth birthday. It's still on the shelf, squeezed
between Dante's *Inferno* and Sharon Olds' *Satan Says.*

Try out the pen first on the back of a bill that claims you owe big time.
Sign your name. As you predicted, the flow stops after the letter E,

followed by a splash the size of a Ritz cracker. Back to the sink
for another flushing. Back to the bottle of peacock ink.

Clean up with a wet paper towel. You are now open for business.
On the first page of the gift journal, the one with textured unlined

beige paper, write the following: "When, if ever, I say this."
Now stop. Admire again the blots and speckles of peacock blue

on your pointer finger and thumb. Hands down, the color peacock blue
has been your favorite, ever since you fell in love with Carolina Chang,

she of the black braids toppled down her back, she who sat
in the desk in front of yours, who showed you her scraped knee—

she whose name you wrote over and over with this very pen,
its ink reminding you not just of peacocks but of things celestial,

of other realms, of the sacred blood of Jesus' twin sister, Veronica,
stuck at home, tending sheep on a mountainside in the clouds.

Once more, fill the balky pen. Pick up where you left off: "When,
if ever, I say this," pausing first to study the nib. You should see

the gleam of ink ready to spell out whatever it is you have been
waiting to say, not knowing, it must be understood,

what that might be. Which is, after all, the beauty of poetry:
the not knowing, the sudden leap into the strange, the realm

of the unexpected. Onward. You're in it now, wading hip deep.
Allow words to river forth. Trust yourself and the leaky pen.

Perhaps this time, there will be no sudden gushes that will drown
your inmost voice. Your subject is a pinecone, your grandmother's

ornate art-deco bracelet from the twenties, a skim of ice
from the pond of childhood, with its glassy mystery and deep secrets.

Your audience is earth and sky. "When, if ever, I say this." Write,
as Dickinson did, your "letter to the world." Only the stars will read it.

Or maybe a few quirky friends who've read Pound and know
poetry is "news that STAYS news." Tell the gods how it goes

with you in words austere, or outlandish—whatever works—
as plain as a spoon, as gaudy as the ink in which that word, *spoon,*

appears on your beige page. Once again: "When, if ever, I say this."
Think of the fountain pen you've brought out of retirement,

alone in the dark, hibernating all those years in a cigar box
with the other pens, waiting for a gleam from the basement light,

patient as the friend you never call, who loves you still.
Imagine the pen as Snow White, comatose but radiant, alive,

ready to be kissed, to snap out of her stupor and start the poem,
beginning with "When, if ever, I say this," and running with it.

GIRL WITH MINT

She has picked a wild fist of it,
lush amid the stream bed thick with rocks
the size of loaves of Italian bread.
Bread rocks, I tell her. She doesn't smile.

Not yet four, she hops from one stone
to another in her purple hand-me-down
sneakers, humming some tune
she invents to the pulse of her steps,

to the tick of water hidden in mint,
curled around the bread stones.
One day not unlike this one, bright
with stream sound, a child's reveries,

the rivery smell of mint, the world
will end. From my seat on a fallen pine,
I study the girl, her mint, a distant snow patch
on the flank of Clemens Ridge.

The old tree bears fire scars, red bark
blackened, trunk uprooted,
delimbed by the fall in our last big wind.
A kingfisher chitters upstream.

I fondle a ponderosa cone picked up,
what – ten minutes ago, or an hour.
The bracts prick my palm.
It's a big cone, female, still closed,

fist-like, waiting to open, to be fertilized
by the smaller male cone's gold pollen.
Humming still, the girl grabs a clump
of monkey flower, purple like her shoes.

I will cherish this moment. From the far side
of Iron Stone Mountain, smoke from a new fire
has begun to spill into the valley. She will not
remember this day. I'll remember for her.

THE TRAIN

He hoists the girl on his shoulders so she can see across the hats
and bonnets. So many people! And so quiet. Why don't they talk?
All them black hats, all them black bonnets! That woman has black
hands. She has never seen a woman with black hands. And the boy
who holds the woman's hand, his hand is black. He got himself some
blue flowers. Why she crying so? Warm sky. Hats and bonnets. The
girl cannot guess where the bumpy sound comes from, a big sound.
Cough! Cough! Train, her father whispers. Be pulling in by and by.
Listen for the whistle. A bell clangs from somewhere. Sad bell. The
whistle – two bursts. She flinches, grips his shoulders. Be coming
directly, he whispers. That there's the steam, Mattie, over the trees. I
can walk fast as that train, Papa. I know you could. Hush now, Mattie.
Red wheels. Stopped. Steam. Big door opens. Men not talking.
Flowers. What's that, Papa, that box? What's in it? Flowers on the
box. Why, Mattie, that's Mr. Lincoln in the box, in his casket. He
sleeping in that box? Mattie, the president is dead. Why's he dead?
Hush now, Mattie. Why that woman crying? She's sad, Mattie. Hush
now. Men close the big door. Whistle blows – she jumps. Bell clangs.
Red wheels. Steam.

~In memory of my great grand aunt, Martha Jane Sharp, 1862 – 1959

REDWINGS

They're hard to spot, woven in wands of reeds,
flashing bits of black between green swords.
Their scarlet epaulets flare like badges of blood.

I want to screech, *zzweee!*, one bird
to another across the marsh, loud
with urgent gossip about mating and food.

On the walk home from the pond,
even when I no longer hear them scold
the sun from the furred, sun-stained

crowns of cattails, I hear them. They feud
still in my mind's marsh. Brash, bold
in their declamations, they berate the gods,

those night-roaming owls who glide
without sound through the wild
forested corners of the world.

The more I listen, the more I understand
Redwing, those arias of breed and feed.
It's not poetry. It may be poetry's bread.

Three Sightings

Dragonfly

Such a tiny biplane, wings of isinglass,
its fuselage translucent blue or green.
You need a pond, lilies, beds of marsh grass
to be a dragonfly, to see and be seen
in glints of colored fire when you pass.
You zig, you zag, lighter than light, careen
non-stop through doors of summer air,
then land on a lily pad and stay there.

Water Ouzel

He bobs his way along the river shore.
The art of nature renders him in slate,
a feathered stone on the river floor.
Wavelets wave to him. They will not wait
as I wait behind a pine to hear the core
of his winged being sing for a mate.
Bright as glass bells over river clatter,
his recitation flows clear as river water.

Barred Owl

For two hours of a fall afternoon
she has not budged from her cottonwood limb.
Dark will drop from Elk Ridge sooner than soon.
(If *she* is *he*, that's okay. So is *they* and *them*.
words mean nothing to the dust of the moon.)
Her gold eyes widen when light grows dim.
Now she blends with the tree's gnarled bark
then, a buffeting of wings in the dark.

~for the grands

All the Horses Have Flown Away

All the horses have flown away.
The bears are sure to follow.
Who knows why koalas play
Or why some trees are hollow?

I saw a wren at the bath today.
It might have been a swallow,
Kinglet, crow or a Stellar's jay,
Or the wings of Apollo,

Whose eyes are made of molten gold,
Whose chariot chases the sky
To let the morning light unfold.
Watch him as he passes by.

Why are leopards black and bold?
I'm certain I know why.
To chase away the wind and cold.
I've seen them, eye-to-eye.

Their sleek backs curve in all my dreams.
They sleep high up in branches.
I've seen them drinking from their streams.
I've seen them move their haunches.

The world is more than what it seems,
Much more than feet and inches,
More than human plots and schemes,
Or purple eyes of finches.

All the horses have gone to bed.
The bears squeeze close together.
Who knows where the wind has fled
Or why each day has weather?

If I could stuff things in my head,
I'd start with a boa feather.
I'd add something my father said
As we waded through the heather.

I don't remember the words he spoke.
I'm too drowsy to recall,
It might have been about the smoke
From bonfires in the fall.

I'm drifting off, so do not poke
While I find my secret stall.
It's raining out, put on your cloak.
It waits for you down the hall.

~for Clio

Not All Horses

Not all horses have green eyes.
Some have silver, some have red.
One I heard of rides the skies.
Another sleeps beside my bed.

You need a horse in times like these
when sad thoughts gallop in your head,
when people's eyebrows make you sneeze.
Your secret horse must be well-fed,

kept warm inside your secret stall.
Your secret horse will not be led
and will not come when others call—
a sign your horse is most well-bred.

Not all horses nicker and neigh.
My horse talks in rhymes instead,
saying words in a special way
words to the world I wish I'd said.

I dream of riding in the dark,
high on a hill where stars are spread
like horses' eyes, each eye a spark
to mark the trail that lies ahead.

~for Hilde

The One Strawberry

She tells you to close your eyes.
You close your eyes.

You feel pressure on your lips—
a textured thing,

red-flavored, sweet, acidic,
a thing with skin.

When you part your lips, when you
suck the thing in—

akin to a kiss – you're blessed
with half sweetness.

The other half she must hold
on her sweet tongue

in this, your shared communion,
one strawberry,

first from the patch you sometimes
fail to water.

June sun fevers your forehead.
Even after

you swallow, your eyes are closed.
Sunlight washes

a wave of fire through your lids.
A berry bit

clings to your lower lip. It's
all you can do

to keep from wiping your mouth.
She steps forward,

presses her hips into yours
and licks it off.

Pika

He's smaller than a rabbit,
larger than a mouse.
He lives in the mountains,
not a house.

His ears are velvet feathers,
his whiskers tiny quills.
Look quick. You might see him
where glacial water spills.

He eats grass and flowers
then hides beneath a stone.
Stream, sky, moonlit spires—
he's never alone.

Walk a skyward path,
the steeper one to where
an alpine meadow lies.
You'll find him there.

~for Cosmo

Goodnight

...and in the streets the blood of the children /
ran simply, like blood of children.
                              ~Pablo Neruda

School's now in session day and night
students sleep
in the classrooms   teachers rolled close
                              ~Adrienne Rich

There is no other way to say this,
        to say what the 4th grade
girl, 11, said, standing
        as she did by the just-opened
classroom door, there with her teacher
        to be greeted by America
in the shape of a young man
        with his birthday gift
to himself, death, his new AR-15.
        Their eyes meet,
teacher and killer by the just-opened
        classroom door.
The 4th grade girl, now and forever,
        must witness
what should never be witnessed.
        You ask: But what about
the glory of rain glistening on leaf ends
        of bamboo?
Or you want to hear about the silence
        of moonlight
on a lake down the road from somewhere,
        a mile or so.

That's not possible, not now, not here
          in the awful privacy
of the public page, not here among
          the broken bones
of these lines. There is no way
          to say this other than
this way, to stand with the 4th grade girl,
          by her young teacher,
by the classroom door opened to a man-boy
          in the shape of America
armed with his toy. *Sweet 4th grade girl I know*
          this is difficult
can you tell us what the man said to your teacher?
          He said "Goodnight."
O Blind God of Rosebuds, Goddess of Paper,
          Scissors and Crayons,
he said to the teacher *Goodnight*
          and pulled the trigger.
There is no other way to say this: He used his toy
          to kill nineteen 4th graders
in their classroom. And with them died
          a word we hear
at the end of every blessed day. *Goodnight.*

~The epigrams above come from Pablo Neruda's poem,
"I Explain a Few Things," translated by Galway Kinnell,
from *The Poetry of Pablo Neruda*, Farrar, Straus and
Giroux, 2003; and from Adrienne Rich's poem, "The
School Among the Ruins," from *The School Among the
Ruins*, W.W. Norton, 2006.

GREAT BLUE
~Ardea Herodias, aka Great Blue Heron

How is it she rises with such grace? I'd walked alone by a pond,
binoculars slung on my neck to bring some living thing—

turtle, bird, river otter, or a red dragonfly – close to my eye.
She had startled me, lifting from her nest of sticks as I passed below.

Or I startled her. I heard nothing but the whoosh of wide wings.
Buffeted by them, swept by their shadow on the path,

a clutch of twigs fell on my shoulder. I tracked her languid glide,
neck tucked in, long legs trailing, to the far end of the pond.

She swooped, back-drafted and settled in a miracle of delicacy
on a log. So still she stood – hunter of shallow waters,

student of waiting and silence – I wondered if what she saw
was what I would see if I had her gold eyes, their black pupils

a pair of moons in eclipse. On her log, before she spears a minnow,
would I – would she – be aware of her reflection, the stylish rake

of her feathered headpiece, the keen edge of her bill?
When I am gone, I understood, after she's caught her catch,

she'll return to the three eggs in her lattice-work nest.
Her world will again become her world. And now,

it's mine as well, altered by my presence, my absence,
before she and I startled each other in a shower of twigs,

before the wind of her wings ruffled my hair and,
in so doing, shifted by a fraction the orbit of the earth.

Squawk
~with thanks to artist Tony Angell for his
public art sculpture, *Emissary Raven #13*

1.
Angell has sculpted his black rock raven in mid-squawk,
the bird's head tipped skyward, beak opened wide.
Winter and summer, I pass his artwork on my daily walk.

This art is no abstract artifact; rather, if you
had spotted the innocuous plaque at the base,
if by chance you'd noticed the near-hidden

sculpture at all, you'd call it true to life, your life.
On closer inspection, you'd see deeper.
You'd say Yes, of course: a stone with lacquered wings.

If I stand still, you'd imagine, it will take to the air,
rise from its pedestal built by a work crew for the city.
Stone, shaped this way, speaks in the tongue of tree and sky,

in the slang of power lines, in the harsh rhetoric
of passing cars. Thus, in my dozen photos of Angel's work,
I crop out cars and lines behind the image of Raven,

who, after all, made this very world, with its cars and lines.
So say the Haida, *Human Beings*. So say the Tlingit,
The Tidal People. Of Raven, the Creator, what they say is true.

2.
Story goes Raven got bored, flying for eons through
the Void. It began to snow. Hard. Well, nothing else to do,
so Raven plays with the snow gathered on his wings.

Tips his wings. This way and that. Up and down.
Snow forms into a little ball. Back and forth the snowball
rolls on Raven's wings. Gets big. After roughly 7000 years,

it's huge! At last, Raven rests on the earth he fashioned
out of snow. He catches his breath, preens a bit,
and plots his next move: to learn the lay of the land—

a daunting task in a darkness blacker than black.
Raven is nothing if not resourceful. And clever.
Too clever, some might say, too much the trickster,

the con artist, often petty, a schemer, driven by pure
curiosity when he spies any shiny thing, possibly edible.
To cite an example, one day Raven stumbles in the dark

upon the tiniest box known to exist, a cedar box
no bigger than a blackberry seed. This tiny box contains
all the light of the universe: sun, moon, stars, galaxies.

3.
Raven pries opens the tiny box. Light pours forth
brighter than any waterfall known to exist.
Lucky for us! Now we can see things: rainbows, orcas,

moss, billboards, forest fires. But where is everybody?
Like the rest of us, Raven yearned for companions,
someone to talk to, a gifted joke-teller, someone

to make up impossible tales that meander off
into the new event called sunset. Story goes Raven
is ravenous, as always – he has been seen accepting

handouts on street corners, pretending to be a blind crow.
On this morning, we see him hop about the cobbles
of a beach on Haida Gwaii, picking fruitlessly

at ribbons of kelp, staring at his reflection in tide pools.
He comes across a fair-sized clam, pries it open and,
more or less by accident, releases all of humanity.

We – our ancestors – had been trapped inside
that cramped, miserable shell – under water except
at low tide – since pretty much the beginning of time.

Out they tumble, squinting in the first sunlight, thrilled
by the sight of trees, birds, mountains. People hug, laugh,
free at last, but with a good-news-bad-news string attached.

4.
That's where we are now. The good news: we're free.
The bad news: we're free to do harm to ourselves, to each other,
to the earth Raven made from snow. There he stands

on his stone perch, still in his bronze tuxedo, among
a few cedars, a lone madrona, a nearby park bench,
a public walking path, the grind of traffic on NE 145th St.

If I didn't know any better, I'd say Raven, his beak wide,
addresses his creation: everything. Whether in protest,
or in a croak of exaltation understood only by his

fellow ravens, or in resigned acceptance of the world as it is,
our emissary Raven welcomes all to this place. Listen.
He squawks his heart out into the blue silence of the sky.

ACKNOWLEDGEMENTS

"At the Curling Rink" appeared in *Triggerfish Critical Review* #26, 2021.

"Bamboo After Rain," formerly titled, "Glass Beads," first appeared in *The Seattle Review of Books,* May 2020.

"Being and Unbeing" appeared in *Nine Mile*, Spring 2022, Vol. 10 No. 1.

Brown Eyes appeared in *Triggerfish Critical Review* #26, 2021.

"Dark Ages" appeared in *Bracken: Poetry, Art and Fiction*, Issue IX, May 2022.

"Deux Rondeaux" appeared in *Vox Populi*, February 23, 2023.

"*Half-Breeds Not Otherwise Counted*" appeared in *Sisyphus Journal: The Next Reality Issue*, fall 2020.

"Holding the Day-Old Baby, I Feel the Feather-Weight of My Death" appeared in *Lights*, published by Pleasure Boat Studio, 2020.

"In the High Sierra" appeared in *Valparasio Poetry Review*, Fall/Winter 2020-2021,Vol. XXII, Number 1.

"Italian Prune" appeared in *Bracken: Poetry, Art and Fiction*, Issue VIII, May 2021.

"Kite: Kalaloch Beach" appeared in *Washington Poetic Routes*, 2019, edited by Claudia Castro-Luna, Washington State Poet Laureate, 2018-2021.

"Midnight Midpoint of the Cedar River Bridge" appeared in *The Madrona Project* #5, spring 2023.

"My Neighbor Hoists a Confederate Flag" is forthcoming from *SALT: Old School Truth and Beauty*, fall 2023.

"My Father's Uncles Doing Time" appeared in *Vox Populi*, July 21, 2022.

"My Father Meets Margaret Bourke-White" appeared in *Vox Populi*, September 20, 2022.

"Oradour-sur-Glane" appeared in *Nine Mile*, Spring 2022, Vol. 10 No. 1.

"Pelicans Diving" appeared in *Vox Populi*, March 7, 2023.

"Pheasants" appeared in *On the Sea Wall*, summer 2022.

"Spring in Hangzhou" appeared in *Triggerfish Critical Review* #26, 2021.

"Squawk" appeared in *The Madrona Project* #4, fall 2022.

"Telling Taurus How It Is" appeared in *Global Poemic*, November 28, 2020.

"The Big Project" appeared in *Sisyphus Journal: The Next Reality Issue*, fall 2020.

"The Last Time" appeared in *Global Poemic*, May 1, 2021.

"The Poetics of Leonard" appeared in *Nine Mile*, Spring 2022, Vol. 10 No. 1.

"The Train" appeared in *Nine Mile*, Spring 2022, Vol. 10 No. 1.

"The Year of the Plague: A Letter" appeared in *The Seattle Review of Books,* May 2020.

"Unable to Waken" appeared in *The Seattle Review of Books,* May 2020.

"Why, for the Third Time, I Failed my Driver's Test" is forthcoming from *SALT: Old School Truth and Beauty*, spring 2023.

"Wild Irises" first appeared in *Under a Warm Green Linden*, Issue 12, Winter 2021-22.

"Winter Solstice: Cormorants Roosting" appeared in *Under a Warm Green Linden*, Issue 12, Winter 2021-22.

SECTION QUOTES:

Section i. Spring:
In spring-time...a song from *As You Like It*, is, like all of
Shakespeare's works, in the public domain.
The trees are coming...by Philip Larkin from "High Windows" in
Collected Poems, edited by Anthony Thwaite, published by Farrar,
Straus, Giroux, 1989, p. 166.

Section ii. Winter:
Tonight as it gets cold...by Mark Strand from "Lines in Winter,"
from Selected Poems, published by Atheneum, 1980, p. 117.
"Breath," by Tess Gallagher, from *Is, Is Not*, published by
Graywolf Press, 2019, p. 99.

Section iii. Fall:
November always... From an 1864 letter by Emily Dickinson
to her friend, Elizabeth Holland.

Section iv. Summer
Hot town, summer...from the song "Summer in the City,"
by The Lovin' Spoonful. Release date: July 4, 1966.
Lyrics by John Sebastian, Mark Sebastian, and Steve Boone.

Section v. Future Spring:
I wake from dreams...by the Song Dynasty poet, Li Qingzhao
(1084-1155), from *As Though Dreaming: Tz'u of Pure Jade*,
translated from the Chinese by Lenore Mayhew and William
McNaughton, Mushinsha Press, 1977. Li is often regarded as
one of the greatest Chinese poets, in the company of the luminaries
of Tang Dynasty poetry: Du Fu, Li Bai and Wang Wei.

AUTHOR BIO:

Edward Harkness has deep Seattle roots. His great-grandmother, Sophia Graff, was born in 1870 near Alki Point, site of the Denny Party landing only 20 years earlier. It's not likely the Dennys and other Seattle founding mothers and fathers could have imagined their beach tents and log cabins as the future home of Amazon, Google and Starbucks. Harkness grew up in Seattle's north end, went to local schools, including the University of Washington, where he wrote his first unpromising poems in classes taught by Richard Hugo, Madeline Defrees, Mark Strand and David Wagoner. Harkness followed Hugo and Defrees back to Missoula and the University of Montana where he earned an MFA degree in Creative Writing. After a two-year stint in the Artist-in-the-Schools program in Montana, Idaho, Oregon and back in his home state of Washington, Shoreline College gave him a crack at teaching writing and literature. That gig lasted 33 years. Harkness is the author of three previous books of poetry, *Saying the Necessary*, *Beautiful Passing Lives*, and most recently, *The Law of the Unforeseen* (2018, Pleasure Boat Studio press). He is the happy, unabashedly proud father of Devin and Ned, both teachers in Portland OR. He counts himself blessed beyond measure to be in love with Linda, his soulmate of 49 years. He and Linda are avid cyclists, gardeners and kayakers in their tandem kayak, fondly known as Big Blue. They live in Shoreline, Washington.